© MOVE ON IN LIFE
BY SANDEEP RAVIDUTT SHARMA

Table of Contents

Foreword IV

MOVE ON IN LIFE....... 1

© **MOVE ON IN LIFE**
BY SANDEEP RAVIDUTT SHARMA

Foreword

This book provides you with a list of 100 motivational quotes and thoughts about LIFE, churned out by my mind with the consciousness, grace and energy of **Shiva Shakti**. I'm sure if you keep reading, referring, sharing these thoughts and quotes about LIFE, you may derive inspiration and develop good understanding of various perspectives and facts. The Ups and Downs in your life are nothing but a way to test your mental resolve. **"Be the reason for someone to smile. Move on in life whether you win or lose."**

I sincerely hope, you will find this book amazing, interesting, rejuvenating, unique and a constant source of inspiration.

Thank You and Happy Reading.

© MOVE ON IN LIFE
BY SANDEEP RAVIDUTT SHARMA

© **Copyright 2018 Sandeep Ravidutt Sharma - All rights reserved.** In no way is it legal to reproduce, duplicate, or transmit any part of this document in either electronic means or in printed format. Recording of this publication is strictly prohibited and any storage of this document is not allowed unless with written permission from the publisher. All rights reserved. The information provided herein is stated to be truthful and consistent, in that any liability, in terms of inattention or otherwise, by any usage or abuse of any policies, processes, or directions contained within is the solitary and utter responsibility of the recipient reader. Under no circumstances will any legal responsibility or blame be held against the author / publisher for any reparation, damages, or monetary loss due to the information herein, either directly or indirectly. The author own all copyrights.

Legal Notice: This book is copyright protected. This is only for personal use. You cannot amend, distribute, sell, use, quote or paraphrase any part or the content within this book without the consent of the author or copyright owner. Legal action will be pursued if this is breached.

Disclaimer Notice: Please note the information contained within this book is for motivational, educational and knowledge sharing purpose only. Every attempt has been made to provide the reader accurate, up to date and reliable complete information. No warranties of any kind are expressed or implied. Readers acknowledge that the author is not engaging in the rendering of legal, financial, medical or professional advice. By reading this document, the reader agrees that under no circumstances the author / publisher is responsible for any losses, direct or indirect, which are incurred as a result of the use of information contained within this document, including, but not limited to, — errors, omissions, or inaccuracies.

If you have further questions, contact on **Tel: +919969256731**
Email: sandeepraviduttsharma@gmail.com

© **MOVE ON IN LIFE**
BY SANDEEP RAVIDUTT SHARMA

Dedication

This book is dedicated to **Shiva Shakti** - the epitome of love. Lord Shiva is pure consciousness symbolising the masculine principle. Goddess Shakti symbolises the active feminine energy of Shiva and is synonymously identified with **Tripura Sundari, Sati** or **Parvati**.

These primal principles are also called as PURUSHA representing consciousness and PRAKRITI denoting the nature. Shiva and Shakti are manifestations of the all-in-one divine consciousness. Shiva is the paternal love of God that gives us consciousness, knowledge and clarity. Shakti is the motherly love of God that showers warmth, care and ensures our protection. Shiva and Shakti exist within each of us as the masculine and feminine energy. To please **Shiva Shakti** praying for the well being, love, happiness, strength, positive energy and success of my readers in their life, I hereby recite the following mantra...

"Sarva Mangala Mangalye Shive Sarvartha Sadhike Sharanye Tryambake Gauri Narayani Namostute"

MOVE ON IN LIFE

© **MOVE ON IN LIFE**
BY SANDEEP RAVIDUTT SHARMA

Move on in life to face the next challenge.

© **MOVE ON IN LIFE**
BY SANDEEP RAVIDUTT SHARMA

Follow your instincts when your knowledge fails.

© **MOVE ON IN LIFE**
BY SANDEEP RAVIDUTT SHARMA

How long would you read success stories of others? It's time to write your own.

Put welcome signs if you really mean it that way.

© **MOVE ON IN LIFE**
BY SANDEEP RAVIDUTT SHARMA

Fly high and see the wonderful world.

Vibrant thoughts break your state of isolation and you become one with the world.

© **MOVE ON IN LIFE**
BY SANDEEP RAVIDUTT SHARMA

Draw strength from goodness and you can never go wrong.

Blind belief cannot show you the way forward.

It's better to forget than remember things or people who don't know what is motivation all about.

Feel the warmth of the fire at a distance or else it can also burn close objects in no time.

Hope likes to live.

The ocean of kindness can do wonders but a drop is sufficient to motivate the depressed soul.

Stay committed in your relationship and live a wonderful life full of trust and togetherness.

Hatred always competes with Love. But love is all about going together.

© MOVE ON IN LIFE
BY SANDEEP RAVIDUTT SHARMA

Fire your ideas towards innovation and you can win.

Let your efforts follow your dreams now.

© **MOVE ON IN LIFE**
BY SANDEEP RAVIDUTT SHARMA

Tour the world not to find happiness but to share.

Before commenting try to understand various perspectives.

Your niceties bring people closer, but your truthfulness makes them trust you, at times even blindly.

The glow on your face tells it all about how much happy you are.

Assuming everything in your life can put you into a dream world. Face the reality and get rid of assumptions.

Motivation works only when you accept your failure and are ready to try again.

Waves of positivity come to your rescue to demolish the illusion of sand castle all along the shore of happiness.

Nothing is difficult in this world if you keep going with a smile.

Take a pause and review your actions if you are not sure of the best way forward.

Self belief is critical for your success in life. You need to train your mind to believe in self before you convince the world.

© **MOVE ON IN LIFE**
BY SANDEEP RAVIDUTT SHARMA

Nothing matters when you have lost hope. With complete surrender, love and devotion to the Lord, you can still remain afloat.

You may search the entire world, but you can find joy only in your heart.

© MOVE ON IN LIFE
BY SANDEEP RAVIDUTT SHARMA

Create Golden moments not to treasure for the future but to live now.

© **MOVE ON IN LIFE**
BY SANDEEP RAVIDUTT SHARMA

Not everyone knows how to thank or appreciate the other. Thanks for your precious time to read this far.

Create and maintain a task queue if you want to complete them in time.

Live in style but not on someone's credit.

Navigate your life into the Sea of challenges not to remain there but to reach the other side of opportunities.

Accept the truth however bitter it may be, as it is thousand times better than false hope.

Wait for the right opportunity only when you cannot create it.

Walk with a candle of knowledge through the dark tunnel of ignorance. Joy awaits you at the other end.

© MOVE ON IN LIFE
BY SANDEEP RAVIDUTT SHARMA

Walk in the rain but still love the Sun.

Don't rush in to read the next chapter of your life before you complete the current one.

The sun never loses its shine after blessing the world. It keeps glowing.

Life is a journey. Sometimes you have to run and at other times treading slowly is the best option.

Things which you do with a focussed mind and from your heart is sure to reward.

To gain knowledge you will have to adopt the recipient approach and be ready to accept the learnings.

Respect never comes out of nothing but something wonderful you have done for the others.

Nothing in this world is permanent. Each one of us is on a mission. Some are aware while others are yet to find the purpose.

Kindness is to help others without any return favour.

Nobody can teach anything to the other unless one is ready to think and listen.

Noble intention is all you need to convince the other.

Attract best of the world by displaying your best behaviour and positive attitude.

Those who try to change yesterday are ruining their today. Live Now.

Citizens of the kind world never let anyone fall.

© **MOVE ON IN LIFE**
BY SANDEEP RAVIDUTT SHARMA

Don't follow your shadow, you never know when the time would change, and it starts following you.

Efforts turn nobody into somebody and lack of efforts again makes one nobody.

Explore new ways with a child like curiosity and enthusiasm.

How you reached your destination is more important than the destination itself.

© **MOVE ON IN LIFE**
BY SANDEEP RAVIDUTT SHARMA

Park your good thoughts into the garage of your mind. Use them when you drive again to make this world better.

Why choose to go through the back door when honesty is your hallmark.

Stay positive even when you don't hear sound of hope. Positivity can light your path and let you go through the darkness of ignorance.

Don't leave everything to your imagination leave some room for the efforts.

Listen to your heart before you queue up for advice.

Let everyone flourish and be happy about it. You will get your share soon.

Move on in life by leaving behind hatred and selfishness.

Those who wish to choose PEACE instead of WAR need to negotiate wisely.

Be brave enough to try again and rise in life.

You can rise in life only when you have self-belief.

© **MOVE ON IN LIFE**
BY SANDEEP RAVIDUTT SHARMA

Sometimes you choose wisely and at times your choice makes you wise.

Congratulate yourself if the world has decided to ignore your win.

© MOVE ON IN LIFE
BY SANDEEP RAVIDUTT SHARMA

Nothing is worth enough to buy your goodnight sleep.

Make efforts to meet your needs and not to fulfill your greed.

Look forward in your life to experience the grace and glory of the #Lord through complete #devotion.

Richness of thoughts can only be felt by a beautiful mind.

Act deaf to System which just speaks but don't do enough on the ground.

Not everyone knows how to express love and likeness for the other.

Most of the time we hardly make attempt to understand others. It is assumed that we are right all the time.

Your dose of Motivation can last longer when it comes from within.

Leave out your problems aside to live an amazing life.

Try to understand what makes you happy instead of figuring out what caused your bad mood.

Waiting tests your patience. Good things in life make you wait. Wait starts right from your birth.

Throw ugly thoughts out of your beautiful mind before they reside to claim ownership.

© MOVE ON IN LIFE
BY SANDEEP RAVIDUTT SHARMA

Don't look for faults but be kind to lift if someone falls.

The beautiful world exist right in front of us. All we have to do is have a look at it and feel good.

© **MOVE ON IN LIFE**
BY SANDEEP RAVIDUTT SHARMA

System which discriminates should be thrown off.

When you keep focussing on your win, you fear to lose. Focus on your efforts and give your best.

Nothing is left to see, when you are acting blind as well as convincing others the same.

How your mind interprets the different situation and thoughts decides whether you will attract positivity or not.

© MOVE ON IN LIFE
BY SANDEEP RAVIDUTT SHARMA

System which steals your livelihood should be abandoned.

Those who have learned to keep patience are sure to win someday.

© MOVE ON IN LIFE
BY SANDEEP RAVIDUTT SHARMA

Focus and complete your task on hand before you decide to pick up the next.

Hungry mind works to create while Angry mind likes destruction.

Don't force others to stay in your life unless they want it that way.

Choices sometimes act as a spoiler and confuses one. If options are available to choose wisely.

Innovations happen when you learn how to expand your limits and think differently.

Nothing else seems to attract your attention when you are in love.

You mind controls the release of both happiness and sorrow. Train your mind to maintain a balance to keep up the value of both.

Never say sorry if you have given your best but still failed. Commit again to bounce back soon.

Stop acting as strangers if you have already introduced to each other.

Rise again in life with joy and leave behind hundreds of bitter falls.

© **MOVE ON IN LIFE**
BY SANDEEP RAVIDUTT SHARMA

See the facts before jumping to conclusions.

Mind always reminds, but heart forgets what's not relevant.

© **MOVE ON IN LIFE**
BY SANDEEP RAVIDUTT SHARMA

Successful people leaves behind trail for others to follow.

Goodness inspires your words and deeds.

www.ingramcontent.com/pod-product-compliance
Lightning Source LLC
Chambersburg PA
CBHW020545220526
45463CB00006B/2193